GOOD MORNING, LORD

Day-Starter Devotions

Robert A. Featherstone

BAKER BOOK HOUSE
Grand Rapids, Michigan

2065081

To My Wife
BETTY
whose love has had
"life-starter" dimensions

1

Meant
To
Thrive

The Kingdom of Heaven
is like . . .
the smallest of all seeds,
but becomes
the largest of plants, and
grows into a tree where birds
can come and find
shelter
(Matt. 13:31, 32, LB).

I'm going to compare you to a moth. But don't worry — it's a comparison that has a built-in bit of encouragement.

The cynthia moth was introduced to Philadelphia in 1861, in order to boost the failing American silk industry. But the moth survives only where its principle food source — a straggly plant called the "tree of heaven" — grows. This tree competes poorly with native trees and shrubs — but wherever the growing is tough, the adaptable plant spreads its roots to find bits of soil to exploit.

In spite of its name, the tree of heaven seems to thrive in the most unheavenly niches. But, where the tree strikes a claim — even among broken bricks and slabs of concrete—the cynthia moth will follow. In fact, researchers have found the largest number of cynthia moth cocoons between the bases of the Manhattan and Brooklyn bridges, among garbage dumps, and in abandoned factories and warehouses. While giant silk moths of other species disappear, the cynthia moth thrives.

I would like to compare that tree of heaven to the kingdom of God, and the cynthia moth to the Christian believer. You see, in the neglected places of our world there is still the possibility of faith. Faith in Jesus Christ seems to thrive in the places where all other ideologies fail. Faith strikes its roots in the most thin and impoverished soil of men's hearts, and for the Christian, there's always the possibility to develop and mature vigorously.

Said our Lord, "Blessed are the poor in spirit, for theirs is the Kingdom of Heaven" (Matt. 5:3, KJV). The tree of heaven is alive today, and thrives in the most adverse situations. Come to its branches for protection and sustenance.

2

All

Undiscovered

My advice to you
is this:
Go to God and
confess your sins
to him. For he does
wonderful
miracles . . .
(Job 5:8, 9, LB).

Childhood is a time to dream dreams. It's a time for fantasizing! As children, we were permitted to use our imaginations, to reach beyond bare reality. But supposedly, when we reached adulthood, we were to readjust our thinking, and engage only in the pragmatic. If that's the case, however, we are impoverished, and indeed to be pitied.

Sir Isaac Newton, the great scientist, wrote before his death, "My life seems to have been only like a little boy, playing on the seashore, and diverting myself now and then in finding a smoother pebble or a prettier shell, while the great ocean of truth lay all undiscovered before me." What a graphic picture of a great truth — we do live on the exciting edge between the known and the unknown!

How are things with you today? Do you feel that your waking hours are filled with boring duties which long ago were reduced to the routine and the predictable? I hope not, because God has built into us the marvelous capacity to see beyond our everyday circumstances.

I like the way the Bible writer Job describes the beautiful possibilities open to the individual who believes in God. "My advice to you is this: Go to God and confess your sins to Him. For He does wonderful miracles, marvels without number. He sends the rain upon the earth to water the fields, and gives prosperity to the poor and humble, and takes sufferers to safety.... He frustrates the plans of crafty men... God saves the fatherless and the poor from the grasp of these oppressors. And so at last, the poor have hope..." (Job 5:8-12, 15, 16, LB).

You see, man is no better than the animals if all he sees in life is what is apparent at the end of his nose. There's a special blessing for the individual who holds on to hope; God loves the one who feels there's a new development around the next corner. So why not adopt the attitude that there's much to learn in life — you can't help but be happily expectant.

3

Riding
Out
Change

Now stand here
quietly
before the Lord,
as I remind you of all
the good things
he has done
for you
and for your ancestors
(I Sam. 12:7, LB).

Tucked away in an old reference from First Samuel are six principles for riding out any storm of change.

The first principle for surviving change is what I call "depend-obedience." In verse seven of chapter twelve, Samuel says, "Now stand here quietly before the Lord, as I remind you of all the good things He has done." Often, our anxiety is a result of forgetting the Lord, or at least forgetting that He wants our well-being more than we do.

The second principle for riding out change is the practice of introspection. A key phrase of I Samuel twelve is in verse 17, "I will pray ... that you will realize the extent of your wickedness." You see, a time of change is an ideal time to develop insights. All too frequently, we are more interested in technological and mechanical novelties than moral growth, which we need far more.

The third principle is the practice of looking around and then looking up. Said Samuel, "Don't be frightened ... don't turn your back on Him in any way. Other gods can't help you" (vv. 20, 21).

Fourth, suggests Samuel, revel in the security of God's love. He describes the care of the Almighty over His chosen people, and says of all that, He did it "just because He wanted to" (v. 22). It is important to discover that when all the familiar is swept away, God's love reassuringly remains.

Fifth, Samuel suggests the principle of confidence in committed leaders. In fact, no other Old Testament character so emphasizes the duty of prayer for others.

The sixth principle works as well now as it did then. It involves letting God's past goodness encourage you in the present. Wrote Samuel, "Trust the Lord ... think of all the tremendous things He has done for you" (v. 24).

In 1968, there was a meeting of ninety social scientists at Princeton University. One speaker was Henry Kissinger, who said, "The biggest lag in our thinking is how to manage change." That's still a problem. But praise God, the Bible offers the key to managing change.

4

Handling Outcasts

The woman
was surprised that a Jew
would ask
a "despised Samaritan"
for anything —
usually they wouldn't
even speak to them! —
and she remarked about this
to Jesus
(John 4:9, LB).

Albinos are people who lack normal skin pigmentation. Society has often ostracized them, but they are creatures in need of tender loving care.

Albinism is a common, widespread genetic disorder. It occurs in plants, insects, fish, reptiles, and mammals, including all human races. The term "albino" comes from the Latin word *albus*, which means white. It was first used in about 1660 by a Portuguese explorer to describe white Negroes he had seen in Africa. Some have even suggested that Noah was an albino. That's because accounts state that his hair was as white as snow, and his eyes like the rays of the sun — the latter possibly a reference to the red reflection of albinos' eyes.

Throughout history, people with various pigment disorders, including albinism, have occupied a spectrum of social positions. Society has considered them everything from outcasts to semi-gods. It's the former that ought to disturb us most. To a lot of people, any feature that's different is cause for ostracism. This kind of prejudice is not noble or admirable in any way — it is no better than what happens in the animal world. A rare albino rhesus monkey, resident of the New Orleans zoo for many years, had to be separated from the monkey colony because of the abuse he received from the more pigmented animals.

When was the last time you or a family member commented adversely about a person who was unattractive, or old, or who was different because of some skin or body problem? Was your comment sympathetic to their difficulty, or mocking of their predicament? Mark 12:31 is evidence of Jesus' attitude. His command was simply, "Love others as much as yourself" (LB). You know what that kind of thinking will do to prejudice or cruel criticism.

5

This Gift
No
Gimmick

But grace was given
to each of us
according to the measure
of Christ's gift.
Therefore it is said,
"When he ascended on high
he led a host of captives,
and he gave gifts
to men"
(Eph. 4:7, 8, RSV).

On their huge reservation in Montana, the Crow Indians had a first-hand experience of modern-day exploitation. As part of a campaign to sell Crow Indians on strip-mining one corner of their land, an oil company displayed a large trailer at the annual fair. Handlettering on the outside of the trailer, which sported the company's emblem, read "Free Movie and Gift." Inside, according to a story in *The New York Times*, the representatives handed out trinkets to visitors, and then showed them a fifteen-minute movie about the wonders and virtues of coal development. According to the report, the film narrator drew an analogy between coal and the American buffalo: The Crow Indians were now being given coal — the "new buffalo," supposedly a new kind of nourishment.

Well, not all the Indians, as you might imagine, reacted favorably. But the oil company's approach was almost as old as man himself. With an advantage to gain, men often use a gift to influence attitude. And I suppose we all have employed the same procedure to secure some benefit.

But the amazing thing is that God reversed this practice when He devised the whole program of redemption. *We* were the ones in need. *We* were lost and came short of heaven's goal. Normally, according to the rules of human behavior, we should have brought gifts to God to try to influence Him in our favor. But I Corinthians 7:7 says just the opposite: "Every man has his proper gift *of God*." Jesus came as the great gift of the Father's heart. What marvelous love! What a revelation of compassion! How good of God to bring gifts to the sons of men!

6

Where The Gospel Excels

. . . the spiritual man
has insight into
everything, and that
bothers and baffles
the man of the world,
who can't
understand him
at all
(I Cor. 2:15, LB).

Have you ever wished that you could grasp the key points of all the world's pagan philosophies? That would enable you as a Christian to point out where the gospel differs from the secular spirit.

I certainly needed that the other day. A hitchhiker was seated in my little Bobcat coupe; and he had just told me that in his view, the Easter Bunny, Santa Claus, and God were all in the same ideological boat. While I was recovering from such a brash and pagan definition of deity, I was reaching for some way to explain his secular spirit. But nothing seemed to come.

Later, I read a book entitled, *Naming the Whirlwind: The Renewal of God-Language* by Langdon Gilkey. In this book, Gilkey assesses the contemporary mind, and lists the following four secular world-views:

First, he says, is the principle of CONTINGENCY. That is the view that all things are caused by forces that are neither rational nor purposive.

Second, Gilkey labels what he calls RELATIVITY. That's the idea that nothing in history is capable of existing by itself. And nothing has any meaning by itself. Everything is dependent, comparative. But if that were true, then God is not absolute, mankind has no source of help outside itself.

Third, Gilkey says, is TRANSIENCE. This is the view that eternity is meaningless and unreal. There is nothing after death. This is perhaps the most devastating idea man can ever entertain. If there's no life beyond this one, then fatalism is our only option. Our lives are purposeless, and the human race merits only pity.

Last, Gilkey suggests, is the principle of AUTONOMY. This is the seemingly logical idea that whatever meaning man has must come from man himself. But in all the centuries of man's existence, no human philosophy of meaning has ever surfaced. How hopeless philosophy is, compared with our hope in Christ!

Perhaps today you'll have a chance to share the simplicity of the gospel. Speak in the absolute assurance that it answers all the questions of the human heart. When Jesus said in John 14:6, "I am the Way," He said it all.

7

You Can
Trust
God

He has given us
both his promise
and his oath,
two things we can
completely count on,
for it is
impossible for God
to tell a lie
(Heb. 6:18, LB).

I recently discovered a delightful thought in a Bible concordance.

Most of you must know what a Bible concordance is. It is like an index of a book, and helps a person locate some specific word, name, or idea in the Bible. It also goes beyond that — serving a broader purpose by grouping ideas on a certain theme together. By using this tool, a Biblical case can be developed on a theme or subject.

Another use a concordance has (and here's where the delightful thought came to me) is to show that many passages and ideas in the Bible are repeated throughout Scripture — either in the Old Testament or the New Testament.

For example, the listing for the word *forgiveness* shows such references as Psalm 130:4, Daniel 9:9, Acts 13:38, and Ephesians 1:7. And the word *hope* is referred to in Job 5:16, Psalm 38:15, Hosea 2:15, and I Timothy 1:1.

So here's my deduction: There is cohesion in the story of redemption; there is uniformity in the divine plan. How good this is in such an important matter as the message of salvation!

In worldly matters, there isn't always such coherence. With so much information available, there's bound to be opposing or at least differing views. One outdoor thermometer says zero, another five above. One group says that a political party is progressive, another group labels the same party regressive. One ad calls a product effective, another ad decries it as a fraud.

Well, we can be sure that when God says something, it's for real, and it's definite. In a world of change and conflicting claims, thank God there's one place for getting truth undiluted — the Holy Bible!

8

Marriage: A Loving Alliance

Show the same
kind of
love
. . .
as Christ showed
to the church when he
died
for her
(Eph. 5:25, LB).

An article in The Royal Society of Health *Journal* pinpointed a problem that every social worker, doctor, or nurse is familiar with — the "battered baby syndrome." But this article went beyond that problem, to spotlight children caught up in their parents' violence toward each other. These are labeled "Yo-yo children," because their emotions and self-images resemble a yo-yo going up and down its own string. Three words used most often by social workers about these kids are: "jumpy, anxious, and nervy." Studies show that children most liked by one spouse are emotionally or physically rejected by the other. Again and again it is evident that the parents use their children as pawns in their marital strife. Associated with all this is restless movement of parents from city to city. In one case, three children under the age of five had been moved twelve times in seven months.

After reading of the plight of "Yo-yo children," I was more convinced than ever that marital counseling is not just for troubled spouses. It ought to be an on-going service to the most happily married couples. A consultancy service has been set up in many cities, but such a service does little good if it is used only at the advanced stages of marital problems.

We need a system of church-sponsored marriage clinics. By this I mean opportunities for spouses to learn the signs of weakening affection, recognize the symptoms of a disintegrating relationship, and take remedial action before the problem gets out of hand.

In the fifth chapter of the Book of Ephesians, Paul compares the marriage relationship to Christ and the church. Notice how many words like "caring" and "loving" suggest repeated efforts to keep the marital ship on course.

"Yo-yo children" are not necessarily all in the non-Christian, "disadvantaged" households. There may be a few in Christendom. But, in any event, every effort must be made to maintain marriage in its Biblical definition — a growing loving alliance. Do something for your spouse today that is Christlike.

9

Dialing
God

O my people,
listen!
For I am
your God. . . .
I want you to trust me
in your times of trouble,
so I can rescue you,
and you can give me
glory
(Ps. 50:7, 15, LB).

Next time you're in a big city, take the phone book and see how many listings there are under the heading "Dial." It's a pretty good indication of the interests and problems in that city.

I was waiting one day for an incoming call in a room at the Shoreham Americana in Washington, D.C. When I glanced down at one of the pages of the Washington telephone directory, I was amazed at the listings under the word "Dial." There was

Dial a Book, Dial a Date, Dial a Dentist, Dial a Devotion, Dial a Dietician, Dial a Discount, Dial a Girl, and Dial a Phenomenon (that clever entry was from the Smithsonian Institute). Then there was Dial a Prayer, Dial a Price, Dial a Ride, Dial a Sermonette, and lastly, Dial your Family Bible.

I don't know if any sophisticated sociologist would buy my idea that such a list is an indicator of the nature of cities. But it does seem to be a cross-section of a city's interests. This city was concerned with dating, dieting, discounts, and devotions. Of that list of thirteen, four had to do with matters of faith, and that's a greater emphasis than on any other subject. And it's true that when we're ready to dial God's way, He's ready to listen to us, and help us whatever the need.

As Jeremiah 29 reveals, "For I know the plans I have for you says the Lord, plans for welfare and not for evil, to give you a future and a hope. Then you will call upon me and I will hear you." So Dial God! We can do it anytime — there's never a busy signal.

10

God's Credibility Never Changes

Heaven and earth
shall disappear,
but my words
stand sure
forever
(Mark 13:31, LB).

A 1930 advertisement for a car produced by the Studebaker Company made some claims which now seem ludicrous. But they illustrate a point about the temporal nature of man, and the eternal life of God.

The ad featured "the dynamic new Erskine Regal Sedan for five people," and read this way: "It's a big car, full 114 inch wheelbase. It's a powerful car, 70 horsepower delivers more power per pound of weight than any other car under $1,000." (Did you notice that price? Read it and weep!) But here's the statement that got me: "Those who can command the best will drive no smarter looking cars than this. Its design is as modern as the dynamic new skyscraper architecture of the day."

Many things that were once called modern and ahead of their time now seem antiquated and even ridiculous. Man, however, is limited to that kind of unreliable judgment because he can only see and perceive in the present. He makes absolute statements based on those perceptions, and has to contradict himself as his perception (or information) changes. He's not clairvoyant, can't predict the future, and hence his judgment is not dependable.

Is this the only life we'll live? Some men say so. God says it is not. Does it pay to have certain standards of conduct? Many people act as if it doesn't. God says it does. Is religion just a crutch for the weak minded? Some philosophers have asserted that. The Bible claims rather that the step of faith is the act of a wise man.

So you see my conclusion. Man can make some very sincere judgments, but in the passing of time his judgments may very well be totally discredited. In view of the light of God's truth given to all who believe in Christ, we ought to say today what Saul said in I Samuel 26:21: "Behold I have played the fool, and have erred exceedingly." Praise the name of the Lord — He takes us back into fellowship every time we acknowledge that we need Him.

11

Quest For Quarks

. . . if you had
faith
even as small
as a
tiny mustard seed
you could say to this mountain,
'Move!'
and it would go
far away.
Nothing would be impossible
(Matt. 17:20, LB).

I have a medical doctor friend who sends me articles and clippings from time to time. A while ago, he wrote me about *quarks,* and the humor of his ideas ought to brighten your day.

My friend noticed an article in *The New York Times* about the effort of scientists to locate the fundamental unit of matter. For, you see, if they could discover the basic building blocks of nature, much that is now a mystery could be explained. So, some researchers have now come up with the quark theory. That is, they have decided to call the (still undetected) basic building block of all matter a *quark*.

After reading the article, my friend wrote a little piece which he called "Quick Quips on Quaint Quarks."

> Have you ever thought of what it would be like to be a quark? Think of the poor little quark, so small that no one has seen him — or her, as the case may be. Just think, a quark may be in your house or on your quilt, and you don't even know it. How does one go about looking for a quark? (A query about a quark will probably produce a smirk.) Are quarks quiet; are they quarrelsome? Can a quark be quoted? Does one quaff a quark? Do they come in pints or quarts? What is the quality and quantity of a quark? Are they quick? I'm quivering with qualms and quaking with questions about quarks. When do quarks have a quorum; a quota? Do they quadruple? I don't like to quibble, so I'll quit making quips on the questionable quark. That should quash further quests for our quarry, the quark."

Well, so much for verbal play; but let me give it all a Biblical application. Our Lord compared faith to the smallest thing His listeners knew, a mustard seed. Today maybe we'd say, "If you have faith as a tiny quark, nothing shall be impossible." Try it!

12

Faith
Needs
Nothing Else

*If they do not hear Moses
and the prophets,
neither will they be
convinced
if some one should
rise from the dead
(Luke 16:31, RSV).*

They're going to try to do a movie translation of the entire Bible. It's not going to be a Cecil B. DeMille spectacular, but it won't be a low budget series either. But will it enhance our understanding of Bible truth? Well, that remains to be seen.

The dream of the British film producer is to make a "film translation" of the Bible. It would be designed for schools and libraries, and would try to present virtually every bit of the Old and New

Testament — all hopefully without interpretation. The producer claims that ours is an age of television in which people just don't read any more, so the movie version will be the people's version of the Bible. Those involved estimate their production will take thirty-three years. The first ten films are ready now, and they'll be offered in a package deal for about $2,000. That also includes supplemental materials like filmstrips, audio cassettes, study guides, and so on.

The films will be simple dramatizations, with some narration, most of it from the King James Version of the Bible. The voice of God, so the producers hope, will be read by Gregory Peck.

Well, how shall we appraise such a production? Will it be an evangelistic tool? Will it revitalize faith? I doubt it. You'll recall that the Lord, in a conversation with the Pharisees, said that people wouldn't believe even if one were to come back from the dead.

The good news of the gospel of Christ is not something that grabs you just because of its dramatic excellence. It's a matter of soul conviction, of seeing one's need for forgiveness, and then of making a total life commitment to the resurrected Christ. Frankly, I hope the film is an aid to faith, but I'm glad we're not linked to the silver screen for any instructions on our eternal destiny.

According to God's design, you can be a happy and productive member of the household of faith with what you know right now.

13

Today's Assignment: Caring

The Christian who is
pure
and without fault,
from God the Father's
point of view,
is the one who
takes care of orphans
and widows,
and who remains true
to the Lord . . .
(James 1:27, LB).

In the fourteenth round of a heavyweight championship match between Joe Frazier and Muhammed Ali the fight was stopped. Yes, the manager called it quits — over the objections even of the fighters themselves. But in that event is a moral for living the Christian life.

The scene was Manila, and Joe Frazier's manager, Eddie Futch, was watching below Joe's corner. He watched the sweat and the water spin off Joe

Frazier's face every time Ali hit him with his right hand. The left eye had already narrowed into a slit, and he was squinting with his right. When Frazier tottered back to his stool after the fourteenth round, Eddie Futch ascertained the condition of Joe's eyesight. Then he simply announced the fight was over. As an article in *The New York Times* put it the next day, "the butchers in boxing wouldn't understand it, but Eddie Futch knew what he had to do." As Frazier's manager he had the right to say and do what he did — and it was all summed up well later when Eddie simply said of the battered Frazier, "There isn't enough money in the world to let him get hurt." I like that fellow feeling. I appreciate someone who puts the care of a friend above dollars and above prestige. Don't you?

Do you understand from your reading of the Scriptures that a Christian is to have that kind of compassion? Take the words of First John 3, "But if someone who is supposed to be a Christian has money enough to live well, and sees a brother in need, and won't help him — how can God's love be within him? Little children, let us stop just *saying* we love people, let us really love them, and show it by our *actions*" (I John 3:17, 18).

I think one of the most effective ways Christians can show their faith in Christ is by actions of kindness and love. If all the world observes is our high-sounding words, we do a disservice to our Lord. After all, He eminently showed in daily action His care for a lost world.

14

Discernment Is the Game

When the Holy Spirit,
who is truth,
comes,
he shall guide you
into
all
truth
. . .
(John 16:13, LB).

You know, it's very easy for foolish ideas to grab us, unless we sift every message we hear through the sieve of common sense and the Bible. When a person is taken in by bad reasoning, he is a loser, both physically and spiritually.

The other day in a Minneapolis department store, I saw a sign poised strategically next to some attractive new shoes which read, "You'll get there on time with such and such a shoe." At first I thought that was a pretty impelling motive for a shoe purchase, but then my logic caught up with me. In what possible way, I thought, could the construction or shape of a shoe help me make an appointment on time? That is a function of my mind — and of advance planning. The feet, after all, just go where they are bidden.

Or take this example. At a large car wash establishment in Chicago, a sign read, "A clean car rides better." Now think that through. Is there even a modicum of truth in it? I grant you a clean car may look better, and the pride of ownership may be enhanced by washing the dirt off. But as for riding — ah, that's pushing advertising claims too far.

My real concern is not with shoes or with cars. It's with the world of the spiritual. In the spiritual realm, we can be just as misled as we can be by exaggerated advertising claims. What sweet nothings, what errors of thinking, what stupid propositions Satan foists upon us! And unfortunately, we often accept his suggestions, only to find out later how faulty our thinking was. Thank God that one of the assignments of the Holy Spirit is to lead us into all truth.

These days, when we are beseiged with as many as 1200 messages a day to buy this, to get that, we especially need to lean on God. We need to be able to sort out truth from error. Discernment is the name of the game, and God's Spirit waits to give it to us today.

15

Life That Is Really New

*When someone becomes
a Christian
he becomes a
brand new person inside.
He is not the same
anymore.
A new life
has begun!
(II Cor. 5:17, LB).*

Let it not be said that religious radio broadcasts don't count for much. They do — both for the broadcasters and the listener. The story of the Totino pizza business is a case in point.

The brand name *Totino* is known all around America. Today, the marketing of that product is a great success. It was not always so. In fact, twelve years ago, Totina Pizza was in deep financial trouble. Back in 1962, Mrs. Rose Totino and her husband borrowed $50,000 to start selling pizzas wholesale. But three years later, the business was operating at a severe deficit. At that time, Mrs. Totino heard a radio sermon by a small Bible college on her car radio. She was convicted of her need for personal faith, and pulled her vehicle off to the side of the road to consider becoming a Christian. As the Associated Press report put it, "she gave her life to Christ." Thereafter, the business took a decided turn for the better. It began to flourish. And not long ago, she sold the Totino pizza business to the Pillsbury Company for $20.3 million. To show her thanksgiving for the Christian radio program, she donated two million dollars to the Bible college.

There's a lesson here — and it is also expressed by the prophet Isaiah in chapter 55, verse 11. He wrote concerning God's Word, "It shall not return unto me void, but it shall accomplish that which I please, and it shall prosper in the thing whereto I sent it." The message of hope through faith in Christ has a miraculous element in it. When a person believes, his life is changed. And God's kind of success always comes on the heels of trusting Jesus Christ. So when you see Totino's pizza in the grocery store, remember a miracle of faith.

16

Holding
Your
Ground

So use every piece
of God's armor
to resist the enemy whenever
he attacks,
and when it is all over,
you will still be
standing up
(Eph. 6:13, LB).

It was just a comment during a small session in a seminary coffee center, but the idea grabbed me. The subject was perseverance.

Dr. Stuart Briscoe of the Elmbrook Church (near Milwaukee) was addressing a group of aspiring ministerial candidates. It was a conference on the ministry, and he shared many good ideas that evening on the Bethel Seminary campus. Here's one that stuck in my mind. Mr. Briscoe said, "An oak is a nut that held its ground." I don't think it was original with him. But what a picturesque way to represent that beautiful quality of determination that sees a project through to conclusion, regardless of the cost.

The term "oak" is the common name for more than three hundred species of trees, all belonging to the genus of the beech family. Considering how small an acorn is, it seems unbelievable that many oaks grow to heights of one hundred feet or more. The brown oak is known for its heavy, fine-grained wood. It was once used in the construction of British merchant ships. Longevity is another characteristic of the oak. Many of the largest English trees still alive were standing during Saxon times. One venerable forest giant, the celebrated Newland Oak, was forty-seven and a half feet in diameter at the time of its destruction. One can only imagine the storms such a tree would weather, the insects it would repel, the blights it would survive. And when you look at an acorn nut, it hardly gives promise of such vibrant and sturdy growth.

That's the way it is in your spiritual life. Looking at faith at the moment of conversion, it seems hardly strong enough to withstand the ravages of life. But the encouraging thing is that Jesus promises to hold His ground, and fan the believer's tiny spark of faith to a consuming flame. Says the Scripture, "I am sure that God who began the good work within you will keep right on helping you grow in His grace until His task within you is finally finished on that day when Jesus Christ returns" (Phil. 1:6, LB).

17

Who Is
My
Neighbor?

*"Now which of these three
would you say
was a neighbor to the
bandit's victim?"
The man replied, "The one who
showed him some pity."
Then Jesus said,
"Yes,
now go
and do the same"
(Luke 10:36, 37, LB).*

I want to applaud something that may revolutionize the burgeoning welfare system. It's called "supported work," and it gives new hope to that large segment of our population who might be called the disadvantaged.

You think the lists are mighty long in the Help Wanted columns of your town newspaper. But there are many individuals who just don't qualify for the average position vacancy. There are millions of

Americans who belong to what might be loosely called the underclass of society. For example, what jobs are there for an ex-convict who has just served twenty years, or for a teen-ager who dropped out of school in the tenth grade possessing no work credentials besides a fifth grade reading level? Or what about an addict who must report daily for his methadone dosage; or a former mental patient who has been institutionalized for five years? Somebody has called them our "civilians missing in action."

An effort is being made to help such disadvantaged people. The program is an adaptation of the "sheltered work" approach developed in the Netherlands and Sweden. It provides subsidized employment to those physically and mentally handicapped persons. A major feature is the conversion of the benefits of the participants on welfare into a salary pool. At last there is a way out of the welfare trap, with public funds going *not* to maintain dependency, but to pay for useful work.

But where does the church of Christ come in? It can take its cue from the story of the Good Samaritan. He not only gave energy and time to help the unfortunate wayfarer, but he used his own money to pay for his night's lodging, with the promise of more if needed. I heard Senator Mark Hatfield say that if each Christian in America would shoulder such a welfare responsibility, we could wipe out a large part of our national debt. 2065081

Obviously, institutions are entrenched in administrative details which often block personal voluntary action. But as Christians, we can love our needy world through Christ, and refuse that self-satisfied apathy which marks the godless affluent.

18

Happy Discovery

*I saw myself
so stupid
and so ignorant
. . .
But even so,
you love me!
You are holding
my right hand!
(Ps. 73:22, 23, LB).*

I wish that the same research being done on the physical life of bald eagles could be done on the spiritual life of human beings. The reason the government is interested in the welfare of the big birds, of course, is because they are among our most endangered species.

The federal government is now asking that a state wildlife agent be notified when a dead bald eagle is discovered. The agent's job is to retrieve the carcass, freeze it, and ship it to a Wildlife Research Center in Maryland. In the last decade three hundred eagles have been so examined, and researchers are finding that poison and gunshot are the birds' persistent enemies.

Have you ever thought about spiritual autopsies? This would help ascertain what brought a human being to despair. I wish somehow we could collect this kind of evidence. What a powerful testimony it would be to the worthlessness of anything that shuts God out.

It seems to me that Psalm 73 is full of such evidence. In verses 3 through 12 the psalmist tells how the wicked flaunt even the idea of God, and refuse to involve Him in their lives. But in verse 17, the psalmist says he understood their end through the help of a worship experience. He saw them in slippery places falling to ruin. He claimed they were destroyed, swept away utterly by terrors.

But that whole sobering passage concludes in a happy discovery when the psalmist says, "But for me, it's good to be near God, I have made the Lord God my refuge" (Ps. 73:28, RSV). If, while we still have life, we can redirect our energies to Christ, then we need not despair again.

19

The Imperative of Now

*The Holy Spirit warns us to
listen to him,
to be careful to hear
his voice today
and not let our hearts
become set against him,
as the people
of Israel did
(Heb. 3:7, 8, LB).*

The opening sentence of the article was, "At long last, we have them, 'Round Tuits,' and we have enough for each of you to have your very own." When I first read this, I dismissed it as nonsensical. I soon discovered, however, that this was a bit of tongue-in-cheek, and the point was one I needed.

The article went on to say, "We have a good supply. Cut yours out and keep it. Guard it with your life. You see, a Round Tuit can answer all the problems of those who've been saying, 'I'll attend church as soon as I get a Round Tuit.' Or, 'Yes, I know my children need the religious instruction of Sunday Bible school, and they'll be there — as soon as I get a Round Tuit.' Others may be saying, 'I'm aware that the Bible contains the good news of Christ's gospel, and when an opportunity presents itself, I'll get a Round Tuit.'" The article concluded by saying, "Won't the new year be wonderful! Now that everybody has his or her Round Tuit, the church will really boom."

Let me suggest that this little bit of serious nonsense concerns the matter of priorities. Obviously, when we say we will get to something later on, it does not claim our first allegiance right now. Many people put off making a decision for Christ. But God doesn't arrange the gift of His salvation that way. Unless through faith you want the help of the Lord *now* in the forgiveness of sins; *now* in the empowering of life to resist temptation; *now* in the reaching for a holy life; unless you want all this desperately *now*, you're risking your spiritual life.

That's the meaning of Matthew 10:37 when Jesus said, "He who loves father or mother more than me is not worthy of me." Don't postpone turning your life over to the Savior until you get a "Round Tuit." It's absolutely a matter of the Here and Now. But verse 39 of that chapter is bright with hope. Said Jesus, "He who loses his life for my sake will find it." And that means right now!

20

How to Neutralize Circumstances

*I am going to
keep on being glad,
for I know that as you
pray for me,
and as the Holy Spirit
helps me,
this is all going
to turn out
for my good
(Phil. 1:19, LB).*

Perhaps you've heard the expression, "To repay good for good is man-like. To repay evil for good is devil-like. But to repay good for evil is God-like." It sets forth quite succinctly the difference in a life style when faith in Christ is present.

In the world of speech and communication, researchers have developed what they call "semantic differential tests." They enable experts to measure a listener's attitudes before and after a persuasive speech. If a good communicator is making the speech, there's usually a marked difference between the "before" opinions of the listener and his "after" opinions.

Similarly, if we know that Christ has forgiven us, and that we now have the power to resist temptation and live victoriously, we can change the most adverse circumstances. We can observe the difference between being overcome and being overcomers.

The best illustration of this I know is the apostle Paul. Take for example the letter he wrote to Christians in the town of Philippi — it's one of Paul's most intimate letters (which is evident by the frequency of the first person pronoun). The dominant note of this little letter is joy. That's all the more remarkable because Paul wrote it from prison. And you see, if that kind of victory happened to one human being, it can happen to you. The message then is clear! The immediate circumstances surrounding a believer's life are not the factors which should determine his attitude.

Are you being pushed around by some financial crisis? Let God help you solve it and live above it. Do you feel disadvantaged, and tempted to be bitter? Let the Lord show you that vengeance is His prerogative; He'll arrange for judgment on the offenders. Are you disappointed by friends? Let Jesus be the friend that sticks closer than a brother. Just remind yourself that because Christ came, we need no more be the victim of circumstances.

21

Make
No
Mistake

Don't be misled;
remember that you can't
ignore God
and get away with it:
a man will
always reap
just the kind of crop
he sows!
(Gal. 6:7, LB).

We all make mistakes at one time or another. Some of them are of no consequence. Others are cataclysmic, and change life's direction.

A common spelling mistake is to spell the second month of the year as we often pronounce it. If we call it "Febuary," we're apt to spell it FEBUARY instead of the correct FEBRUARY. Or take the word that means "lacking in life, spirit, or zest." Some pronounce it LAXadaisical, but actually there's no such word in the dictionary. There's the word LAX, and then there's the word LACKadaisical, but you can't combine the two.

In the world of the spiritual, similar mistakes are often made. The consequences for these errors, however, are almost always serious, if not tragic. Take the idea that there isn't really any God. This idea would seem logical, because nobody has seen Him or heard Him or touched Him. But the Bible calls anyone with this notion a fool (Ps. 14:1). God does exist, and just because we can't perceive Him with any of our five senses doesn't change the fact of His existence at all.

If you approached one of the many great scientists out at Los Alamos, and said, "I have never in my life seen an atom, so I don't reckon there is any such creature," they'd be kind if they didn't laugh in your face.

Or take the matter of the Holy Spirit. The Bible says He personally comes to live in the life of the believer in Jesus Christ. He serves a very vital function. He guides into truth, convicts of sin and wrong; and serves as a counselor when life gets perplexing. He continually provides a guarantee that once we turn our lives over to Christ, we're in His family for good, and heaven is our beautiful destination. Again, our senses can't prove these things, but that doesn't mean they're any less true.

Don't make a fatal spiritual mistake and cheat yourself out of all God wants to give you.

22

In Praise
Of
Common Sense

I am sending you out
as sheep among
wolves.
Be as
wary as serpents
and harmless
as doves
(Matt. 10:16, LB).

It's time to say something in the praise of common sense! Somebody has said that "Common sense is of all kinds, the most uncommon." But if we don't use it, neither God nor men can help us.

Let me use an example of common sense from the New Testament in a way you've perhaps never heard it applied. You know of Stephen, the martyr, whose story is in the sixth and seventh chapters of Acts. The Jewish leaders were upset at the evangelistic efforts of the Christians. They were particularly angry at Stephen. They claimed he had used blasphemous words against Moses and God.

So the Sanhedrin was convened. And Stephen was allowed to speak in his own defense. What did he do? He embarked on a long extract from Israel's history. It starts in chapter 7, verse 2, and goes on through hundreds of words to verse 50. Why did he do that? Part of the reason was to appeal to the fact that God reveals Himself in history. But the other reason certainly was to gain himself a hearing for his message. He used common sense. He knew that the judges could not cut short a summary of their own sacred history! Beautiful common sense.

Now, God has given us minds. And supernatural help notwithstanding, we're to use our minds. Said Henry Ward Beecher, "If a man can have only one kind of sense, let him have common sense. If he has that, and uncommon sense too, he is not far from genius." Said another, "It is not enough to do the right thing, it must be done at the right time and place. Talent knows what to do, common sense knows when and how to do it."

Pray today for a sanctified common sense.

23

Taking
The Long
View

*I know the one
in whom I trust,
and I am sure that
he is able
to safely guard
all that I have given him
until the day
of his return
(II Tim. 1:12, LB).*

Have you ever transferred fish from one bowl to another? You know how the fish struggle in the net, as if they were being removed from the water forever. They just don't realize that the purpose of their own temporary discomfort is to give them a better environment. Just so with us. We grind under adverse circumstances — unless, that is, we can take the long view of life that the Bible gives.

I think all of us want to have that enviable attitude about life that refuses to be caught in the pessimism of the moment. We want to believe that ultimately, faith in God will show that *everything* can work for good. And of course, that's Paul's message in Romans 8:28. He articulates that idealism, that optimism, which is at least potentially in all of us. The Bible teaches that faith lifts up the head of the believer, because it asserts that redemption is always drawing near. Do *you* believe that? Do *you* know that today, as a follower of Christ, you are one step nearer to that moment when you'll be ushered into the beautiful world of His kingdom?

A person who learns to love God realizes that all experiences are animated by a divine purpose of good. A poet, on the subject "It Is Well" put it this way: "And thus, while years are fleeting, though our joys are with them gone, In thy changeless love rejoicing, We shall journey calmly on. Till at last, all sorrow over, Each our tale of grace shall tell, In the heavenly chorus joining, LORD, thou hast done all things well."

If you realized you would say that to Christ one day, you wouldn't be so uptight about today's trouble.

24

The Pleasure
Of Being
Upright

My Holy Spirit
shall not leave them,
and they shall
want the good
and hate the wrong —
they
and their children
and their children's children
forever
(Isa. 59:21, LB).

Paul put it well when he said in Ephesians 6:13 that the Christian would come upon situations when all he or she could do was to stand fast. In situations like these, aggressive action is not possible, and the attack seems almost overwhelming. But right then, we can count on God's help to enable us to hang in there, and not capitulate to the enemy of our souls.

Not many realize all the temptations people face

on the job. Take a supermarket for example. The cashier may be pressured for discounts, maybe the market manager can be persuaded to reduce the price on an item. A maintenance man may be tempted to use company equipment for his own or a friend's needs. Or the accountant may be tempted to force a cash balance in order to divert attention from a shortage. Or maybe the manager contrives to give more display space for a little kickback from the supplier.

Well, you know what kinds of temptation you face, and you know how difficult it is to stay honest. We live in an era of what is called "situation ethics," which simply means that many people's moral standards arise out of the expediency of the moment. Even though history shows that society has inevitably gone down to ruin with such a system of moral conduct, man keeps trying it.

The apostle Paul said, "Having done all, to stand" and then he explains how that is done. He talks about having truth, about practicing righteousness, about taking the shield of faith and the helmet of salvation, about praying and keeping alert.

I'm suggesting to you today that you hang on to Christ and the moral fibre you have; don't let the devil fast-talk you out of the pleasure of being upright.

25

Unity In Diversity

Under his direction
the whole body is
fitted together perfectly,
and each part
in its own special way
helps the other parts,
so that the whole body
is healthy
and growing
and full of love
(Eph. 4:16, LB).

The church is the only institution that knows no limitations of race, class, power, or privilege. It's a family rich in diversity, where variations only accentuate commonality.

In the Epistle to the Ephesians, Paul told his audience that the Christian church was to be thought of as a body. The church is one great organism, where each member shares a common dynamic. This is true even though external characteristics differ greatly.

We Christians sometimes have a hard job accepting our differences. But God has built such stupendous differences into the rest of His creation that they constitute a good object lesson for us in the principle of unity in diversity.

Take, for instance, the mammals. They are members of a biological class which is warm-blooded, hairy, and which nourish their young with mother's milk. But mammals are incredibly diverse. They range from the blue whale to the pigmy white-toothed shrew.

The blue whale is the largest living mammal, with a record weight of 134¼ tons. The heart of the whale is so large that it takes seven men to drag it over the deck of a whaling ship. The great tail fin, or flukes, of this whale can propel it to speeds of twenty knots.

The pigmy white-toothed shrew is also a member of the mammal family. It is found along the Mediterranean coast, and averages in weight about two grams. The size ratio between the upper limits of whaledom and the lower limits of shrewdom is about 100 million to one. But molecular bio-physicists say that each have the same overall body plan, and undergo the same type of developmental process from fertilization to birth.

If God can arrange the class of mammals with such diversity, He can also design startling variety in His choice creation — the Christian church. Unfortunately, we spend a lot of time trying to make everybody fit one mold. However, if a person is surrendered to the will of God and possesses a life-changing faith in Christ, then diversity is not a drawback. In fact, it can be a source of great strength.

26

Good Advice

Don't criticize,
and then you won't
be criticized.
For others will treat you
as you
treat them
(Matt. 7:1, 2, LB).

If you had been able to drop in on this conversation between a married woman and her minister, you might have gotten an insight or two.

Said the wife: "After talking to my husband, can't you see that he is just a little boy who has never grown up?" Pastor: "Well, he has some real problems, but you will have to admit that he holds a pretty good job." Wife: "Yes, I know, but Pastor, he's just a big baby. Look at the way he acts when my brother comes to see me. You would think that my brother is an old boyfriend." Pastor: "That burns you up doesn't it?" Wife: "I have just never seen anyone as jealous as he is. He just wants to possess me, body and soul." Pastor: "Tell me, how do you figure this? How did he get that way? You must know a good deal about his childhood." Wife: "Oh, yes, he was a spoiled child, and always had his own way. His sister and his mother waited on him hand and foot. And now he expects me to do the same."

Pastor: "To me the problem seems to be a very critical one. He seems to need more than you can give, and becomes angry when you do not meet his demands. On the other hand, the only approach you have found is to judge him, to call him immature. Is there no other approach to this problem?" Wife: "Is that what I'm doing? Judging him?" Pastor: "It seems so to me. You seem to have lost respect for him, to think of him as immature, as a little boy. Isn't that judging him, in a way?" Wife: "I guess that is judging him."

While I don't know what further counseling the pastor provided, I think he well might have used the statement of Scripture above in Matthew 7. Or, he might have used verse 12 of that same chapter: "Do for others what you want them to do for you."

27

Getting Forgiven

Create in me
a new, clean heart,
O God,
filled with clean thoughts
and right desires. . . .
Restore to me again
the joy
of your salvation,
and make me willing
to obey you
(Ps. 51:10, 12, LB).

One hardly speaks of sin any more. That's too bad! I wish we had some of the concepts on sin in our sophisticated age that most people accepted back in the Middle Ages. It could be a real step ahead for us.

People in the Middle Ages were conscious of three special sins that drove a wedge between man and his environment. The first was the sin of *pride*, which the ancients said would separate man from

God. Pride, of course, was the original error of the devil, and it caused him to be cast out of heaven. The second sin spoken of in the Middle Ages was *envy*, which was described as separating man from his neighbor. If your neighbor's possessions or status caused you to become jealous, obviously you would not be on good terms with him. And lastly, they spoke of the sin of *anger*, which separated man from himself. When angry, a man is not in control of himself; he is not keeping his passions in check. So there is the evil triumvirate — Pride, Envy, and Anger — three deadly sins that move man away from God, from his neighbor, and ultimately from himself.

With that background, you can now better appreciate the words of Paul to Timothy, the first epistle, chapter 6, "Oh Timothy, you are God's man. Run from all these evil things and work instead at what is right and good, learning to trust him and love others, and to be patient and gentle. Fight on for God" (I Tim. 6:11, 12a). I would imagine that Timothy responded favorably to *that*.

We need to hear this message again today. Many of the non-fiction books on the best-seller list have to do with selfish aggrandizement: how to develop and use power, and how to win by any and all means.

Think what would happen to our society if a major segment of our people renounced the sins of pride, envy, and anger. Why, a sort of millennium would be ushered in! But you and I shouldn't worry about the rest of the crowd. If we would allow God's power to do this in our own lives, I believe we'd turn the tide.

28

Life,
Not
Death

The thief's purpose
is to steal,
kill,
and destroy.
My purpose is
to give life
in all its
fullness
(John 10:10, LB).

Are you aware that abortion is not a phenomenon limited to the United States?

In no way am I a supporter for abortion. I leave that subject for evaluation in another place. But there's an aspect of that whole subject that says something about any idea whose time has come. I do want to make two observations about abortion, based on an article in *The New York Times*.

No democratic nation, once having liberalized

the abortion law, has ever returned to more restrictive laws. Apparently, two-thirds of the world's population now live in countries permitting relatively easy access to legal abortion. Five years ago, it was only one-third. (This observation is based on a study financed by the United Nations.) It is clear, therefore, that we need to watch the philosophy our lawmaking reflects; once we start whittling away at the so-called restrictions of the past, we have then no more standards by which to gauge our actions. How desperately we need the laws of God, those holy standards by which human conduct can be measured!

The authors of the *Times* study claim that few social changes have ever swept the world as rapidly as the legalizing of abortion. How sad; it indicates that man has latched on to an idea that destroys life with an enthusiasm he has never given to an idea that creates life.

Christianity (the most perfect example of a life-creating idea) came on the world scene to give man hope, to provide spiritual light in place of pagan darkness. If any idea should have swept the nations it should have been this one, but we've resisted it. We've relegated it to the interiors of sanctuaries; we've ghettoized it in the homes of suburbia.

What would it mean to the world if the life-giving message were to be as eagerly sought as the death-dealing one?

29

Genuine Freedom

So if the Son
sets you
free,
you will indeed
be
free
(John 8:36, LB).

Freedom is a beautiful word. And you would think that with all the wars fought to assure it, and with all the blood spilt to acquire it, the abuse of freedom would have disappeared from the face of the earth. Sadly, this is not so, and East and West Germany provide a case in point.

For many years now, the West German government has been quietly paying up to $15,000 a person to *buy* the freedom of prisoners in East German jails. Those payments are raw reminders of the inhuman aspects of the partitioning of Germany. The continuing cold war antagonisms still exist, despite a 1972 treaty that improved relations between the two countries.

According to a *New York Times* report, some of the persons brought out of East German jails are chosen to reunite divided families. More frequently, however, the basis for the selections is simply the caprice of the East German officials. As far as we know, there is no quota, so the number of persons allowed out depends on the amount of West German marks that the East Germans need for their international trade at any particular time. This kind of trade in human beings is evidence of the inherent fallen nature of man.

But the second chapter of First Samuel in the Bible (part of Hannah's prayer) speaks of God's concern for all men. "He lifts the poor from the dust, yes, from a pile of ashes, and treats them as princes, sitting in the seats of honor. For all the earth is the Lord's and He has set the world in order, He will protect His godly ones."

Any time the view from the human perspective is disappointing — yes, despairing — try the view from the cross. Christ's sacrifice at Calvary is the world's one great event that chases bondage and establishes freedom forever.

30

Jesus

As

Light

His life is
the light that shines
through the darkness —
and the darkness
can never
extinguish it
(John 1:5, LB).

The statements of Christ are often confirmed by the scientific discoveries of men. One such perceptive statement of Jesus concerns light.

For as long as man has been around, the importance of his eyes has been taken for granted. But research shows that beyond the function of sight, the eyes play an important part in emotional stability.

The poultry industry has long known that you can increase egg production by lengthening the short daylight hours of winter with artificial arc lights. The eyes here play a role beyond the mere visual function. You see, eyes act as photo-receptor mechanisms, affecting the neurological system as well. The hens' response, therefore, is caused by light entering their eyes and stimulating the pituitary gland.

Likewise in the human eye, light responses go beyond the range of human vision. There are invisible rays at either end of the spectrum — some beneficial and some harmful. Take TV for example. In tests, radiation from TV sets were found to cause nervousness, continuous fatigue, headaches, loss of sleep, and nausea in a group of students who watched TV three to six hours each weekday and six to ten hours on Saturday and Sunday. Later, total abstinence from television made all these symptoms vanish in two to three weeks.

Consider then the statement of our Lord in John 8: "I am the Light of the world" (v. 12). It certainly means more than just to explain His divine role in shedding light on heretofore hidden subjects. For, just as the light in human eyes affects moods and emotions, so the light of Christ's gospel provides us with more than just eternal life — things like peace, joy, and hope. Jesus as the light — what a beautiful metaphor of His vital importance to each of us.